LEARN ABOUT Global Warming

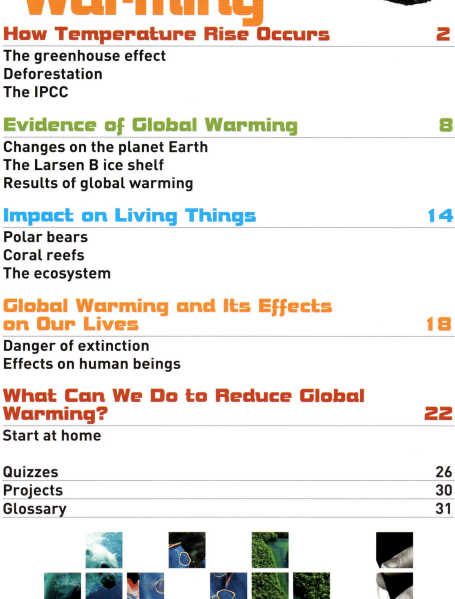

How Temperature Rise Occurs	**2**
The greenhouse effect	
Deforestation	
The IPCC	
Evidence of Global Warming	**8**
Changes on the planet Earth	
The Larsen B ice shelf	
Results of global warming	
Impact on Living Things	**14**
Polar bears	
Coral reefs	
The ecosystem	
Global Warming and Its Effects on Our Lives	**18**
Danger of extinction	
Effects on human beings	
What Can We Do to Reduce Global Warming?	**22**
Start at home	
Quizzes	26
Projects	30
Glossary	31

How Temperature Rise Occurs

Global warming refers to an increase in the planet's average surface temperature. Natural and human causes have been suggested to explain this phenomenon.
The rise in temperature of the past 50 years is most likely due to an enhanced greenhouse effect, caused by an increase in greenhouse gas concentrations in the atmosphere.

THE GREENHOUSE EFFECT

The Earth's atmosphere traps part of the sun's energy, keeping itself at an average temperature of 13 °C (55.4 °F). Meanwhile, the Earth's surface and the clouds reflect the other part of this solar radiation. This natural phenomenon causes what we call the greenhouse effect, and without it there would be no life on land and in the oceans, at least not life with the current diversity and degree of complexity.

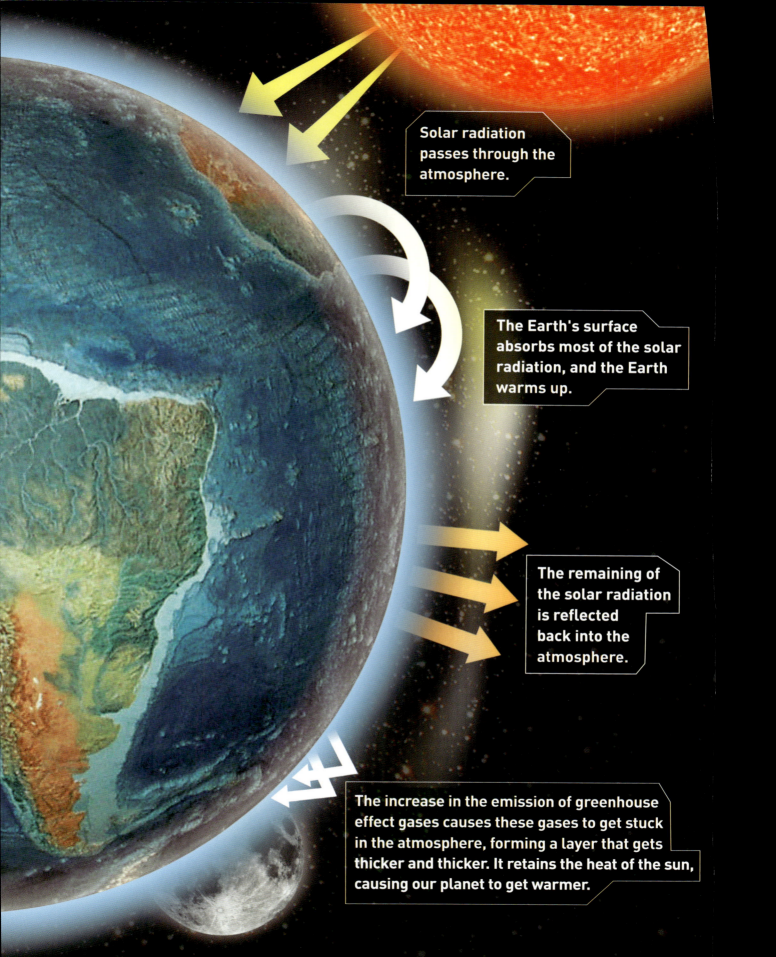

It is important to remember that the greenhouse effect is a natural phenomenon on Earth. It becomes an environmental issue when the emission of greenhouse gases – such as carbon dioxide, methane, chlorofluorocarbons, and nitrous oxide – begins to rise because of human influence.

The increase in the concentration of these gases causes the average global temperature to rise, and this is known as global warming.

The increase in CO_2 is considered the main factor in global warming because it represents 60% of the gross volume of greenhouse gas emissions. CO_2 remains active in the atmosphere for approximately 100 years and it traps the solar radiation reflected by the planet's surface, thus making Earth warmer.[1]

THE MAIN GREENHOUSE GASES THAT CONTRIBUTE TO THE INCREASE IN THE AVERAGE GLOBAL TEMPERATURE ARE METHANE, NITROUS OXIDE, CARBON DIOXIDE, AND CHLOROFLUOROCARBONS. WHERE DO THEY COME FROM?

CH_4 METHANE
- Landfills
- Decomposition of organic matter
- Combustion of natural gas, coal, and petroleum
- Cattle farms
- Rice plantations
- Wetlands

N_2O NITROUS OXIDE
- Combustion of fossil fuel and plant matter
- Use of fertilizers
- Industrial processes

CO_2 CARBON DIOXIDE
- Respiration of living things
- Decomposition of plants and animals
- Forest fires
- Combustion of wood, coal, petroleum, and natural gas
- Deforestation
- Cement production

CFCs CHLOROFLUOROCARBONS
- Refrigeration systems and aerosol sprays

DEFORESTA...

... is another contributing factor to the greenhouse effect because trees absorb carbon dioxide from the atmosphere. This natural process – CO_2 absorption by the

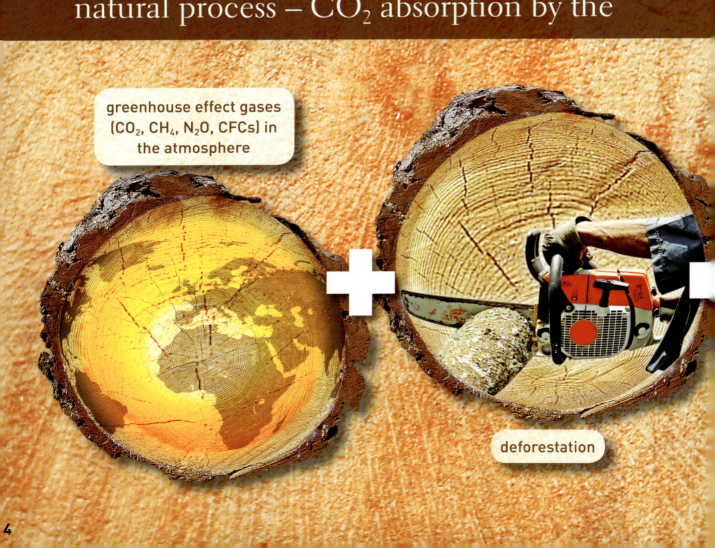

greenhouse effect gases (CO_2, CH_4, N_2O, CFCs) in the atmosphere

deforestation

TION...

trees (and other living things) – is known as photosynthesis. During photosynthesis, carbon dioxide is absorbed and oxygen (O_2) is given off to the atmosphere.

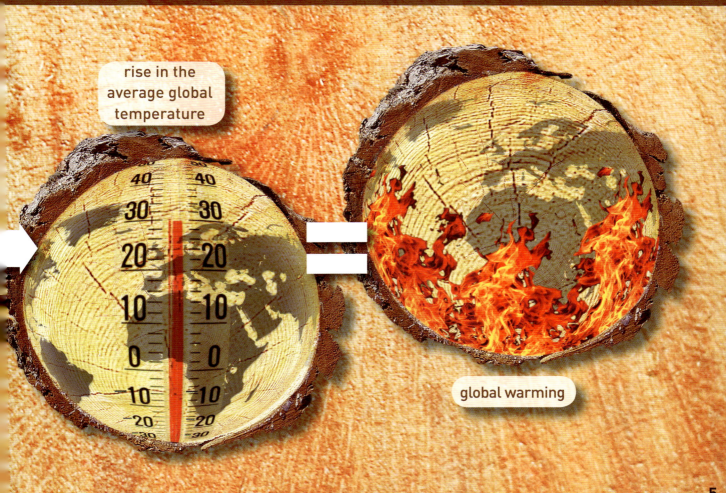

rise in the average global temperature = global warming

The IPCC

(Intergovernmental Panel on Climate Change) wants the world to understand that the warming observed in the past 100 years is due to human influence and that the average global temperature will be increased in 0.3 °C to 4.8 °C by the end of the century.[2] Industrialized countries are this planet's main polluters. Here are the top five CO_2 emitters *per capita* in the world:

		CO_2 EMISSION IN TONS PER YEAR
1	Qatar	40.3
2	United States of America	17.5
3	Australia	16.9
4	Canada	14.6
5	Russia	12.2

[3]

Even though the global warming issue has been in the media headlines lately, it is not a new problem. Climate change started with the formation of the planet. The scientific community has been monitoring these changes for many decades. During the last 30 years, however, organizations have been created, conferences have been held, and protocols have been signed in order to deal with this issue.

THE UNITED STATES OF AMERICA, ONE OF THE COUNTRIES WITH THE LARGEST EMISSION OF CARBON DIOXIDE in tons per year, withdrew from the Kyoto Protocol in 2001, claiming that the treaty hurt its economy and unfairly benefited developing countries.

1987
46 countries signed the **Montreal Protocol**. As an attempt to protect the ozone layer, it tried to reduce the production of several substances responsible for depleting the ozone layer, including CFCs.

1988
The World Meteorological Organization (WMO) and the United Nations Environment Programme (UNEP) established the **Intergovernmental Panel on Climate Change** (IPCC). The IPCC looks at human activity and evaluates its risk on climate change. The IPCC doesn't conduct research but it does publish reports, usually from published scientific literature, on the status of global warming on our planet.

1997
The **Kyoto Protocol** required industrialized countries to reduce their overall emissions of six greenhouse gases to 5.2% below 1990 levels. They would do this between the years of 2008 and 2012. One of its relevant aspects is the fact that only the Annex 1 parties (Australia, Canada, European Union – France, Germany, United Kingdom – Japan, Russia, and the United States of America, among others) are committed to reducing their greenhouse gas emissions. Developing countries such as Brazil, China, and India, major emitters of pollutants, are encouraged to participate in emissions abatement activities, but do not have emission targets like the Annex 1 parties.④

2012
In a conference celebrated in Doha, Qatar, nearly 200 nations agreed to extend the Kyoto Protocol to 2020. Nevertheless, the deal covers Europe and Australia, whose share of the world's greenhouse gas emissions is less than 15%.⑤

GLOBAL WARMING is related to an increase in the concentration of greenhouse gases in the atmosphere. This increase is directly linked to certain economic activities, especially in the areas of energy, transportation, and forest management.

Evidence of Global Warming

There is no doubt that global warming is raising the Earth's temperature. What impact will this phenomenon have on our planet?

We can feel the effects of global WARMING all over the planet: summers are warmer and winters are shorter and not as cold.

2010 was the warmest year in the last three decades, with an average TEMPERATURE of 14.59 °C. The second warmest year in this same period was 2005, with an average temperature of 14.58 °C. The average temperature in 1998 was 14.56 °C, the third warmest.[6]

The rising temperatures are causing valley glaciers to MELT. These hold 9% of the planet's freshwater supply. As a result, sea levels RISE, and there is less water for human consumption and use in agriculture.

Besides posing a threat to our water SUPPLY, the melting of valley glaciers causes serious problems such as landslides and floods, threatening the lives of the people who live in these areas.

Continental GLACIERS in Antarctica and Greenland are also melting. These glaciers hold another 70% of the planet's freshwater reserves. During the summer, portions of melting glaciers break off and move slowly to the sea.

We can see the effects of global warming on the **ANTARCTIC PENINSULA,** where most of the **Larsen B** platform has collapsed. This ice shelf has lost an area of

9,800 km²

in the last 20 years.[7]

IT'S IMPORTANT to pay attention to these disintegrating ice shelves...

THIS SEQUENCE OF NASA satellite images shows the disintegration of the Larsen B ice shelf in 2002. It lost an area of approximately 2,500 km² in a 35-day period.

...IT'S A SIMPLE EQUATION:

a warmer planet **melting ice** **rising sea levels**

Heat waves cause parts of Europe to dry up and become more vulnerable to fire. The opposite is also happening: the warmer water temperatures have already caused an increase in precipitation. This increased precipitation may have been the cause of recent flooding in southern Germany and Switzerland.

Sea levels may rise between 29 and 82 centimeters by the end of this century. That is enough to threaten the existence of places such as the Pacific Islands, Holland, and Belgium, among others. [8]

In Ethiopia, annual droughts contribute to the famine suffered by over 6 million people.

While global warming is causing floods, melting ice shelves, and rising sea levels in some parts of the world, some other parts are undergoing severe droughts.
The number of regions affected by droughts has doubled over the past 35 years. ⑨ Now deserts cover over a quarter of the Earth's surface. In China, desertification is spreading at a rate of 10,000 km² per year. This is an area the size of the country of Lebanon.

Hurricanes are another way we can see the dramatic effects of global warming. In the past 40 years, the average ocean temperature has risen by 0.5 °C. This increase causes more water vapor to form and provides extra energy to feed hurricanes. As a result, there has been a noticeable change in the frequency, intensity, and course of categories 4 and 5 hurricanes. In a category 4 hurricane, the wind blows between 210-249 kilometers per hour, and in a category 5 hurricane, these winds move faster than 250 kilometers per hour. ⑩

Hurricane Rita in Cuba

Hurricane Katrina in New Orleans, USA

Most of the recent catastrophes we've heard about in the news are due to climate change. Floods, tornados, hurricanes, and droughts have been changing lives around the world.

Impact on Li

THE EFFECTS OF GLOBAL WARMING can be seen on land, water, and air, and they threat the existence of several species. According to the IPCC, 20-30% of the Earth's living species will be in danger of extinction if the planet's average temperature increases between 2 °C and 3 °C over the average temperature of the year 1990. [11]
POLAR BEARS and **CORAL REEFS** would be the first victims of global warming.

POLAR BEARS can be found in Alaska, Greenland, Russia, Canada, and the Norwegian Islands. But polar bears are in trouble. In the Arctic region, climate change is happening twice as fast as it is on the rest of the planet. As the sea ice on which they live melts, the polar bears' hunting territory diminishes, and this poses a serious threat to their existence.
Another lethal problem is drowning. Even though polar bears are excellent swimmers and able to swim great distances, they need to rest on ice blocks along the way. Since these blocks of ice are becoming scarce, the polar bears drown.

ving Things

MANY KINDS of organisms are part of the coral reef ecosystem. Some of the most important are the algae, that provide nutrients for the coral polyps, tiny individuals that live inside corals. When the water temperature rises, corals expel these algae and start to look like white skeletons. We call this phenomenon **coral bleaching**. The algae are also involved in the calcium production that forms the coral skeleton.

The Great Barrier Reef stretches more than 2,200 km along the northern coast of Australia. It has already recovered from two major **coral bleaching** events.
However, scientists are concerned that the Great Barrier Reef may not be able to recover from future bleaching events, especially if water temperatures continue to rise.[12]

Global warming also threatens other species...

Global warming can also provoke significant changes in vegetation zones and poses a serious threat to biodiversity.

The Amazon Rainforest, one of the world's largest tropical rainforests, is likely to witness a significant drop in humidity levels. Its dense equatorial vegetation could be replaced by plains with scarce vegetation. A change in the Amazon Rainforest's ecosystem would not only cause the extinction of several plant species, but also a massive extinction of animal species.

Even though it's impossible to prove that the environmental changes we are witnessing are due to global warming, there is strong evidence available that it's true. In fact, there is no other reasonable explanation. And it's not likely that the changes we are witnessing are random.

Increased levels of CO$_2$ concentration cause water to become more acidic. This causes the destruction of the external shells of **mollusks**. When CO$_2$ is absorbed by water, it forms a weak acid known as carbonic acid which can destroy the shells, thus threatening several marine ecosystems.

Global climate change may also cause a depletion in the nutrients available in the upper layers of the ocean. This means a reduced **phytoplankton** population and a consequent reduction in the populations of fish that feed on phytoplankton. That means less food for all of us.

An increase in the acidity of the ocean waters also makes it difficult for fish to breathe. As a result, large fish populations may die out. Further, **acidic water** affects the reproductive systems of some species of fish.

Some species of whales may also become extinct due to global warming because they eat **krill**, a small crustacean. The krill population is dropping dramatically because of increased ocean temperatures and acidity. This is hurting not only the krill, but also the mammals that feed off them.

Mangroves are natural nurseries and guarantee the replacement of fish populations. But floods caused by increasing sea levels are destroying mangrove forests and causing reduced fish populations.

Global Warming and Its Effects

Are human beings in danger of extinction?

HUMAN BEINGS, like all other mammals, have a mechanism which helps us to maintain a constant body temperature. We have also developed the technology necessary to control room temperatures so that it doesn't matter if it's too hot or cold outside. Is it correct then to assume that global warming will have no impact on us? Not at all!

on Our Lives

AN INCREASE in temperatures around the globe can also have a direct impact on the survival of cold-blooded species. These animals, whose body temperature changes according to the temperature of the surroundings, are already suffering from climate change. The golden frog is one of the animals that became extinct since there was no place for it to go in order to escape the warmer temperatures.

Unless we change the current trend, global warming will also affect human beings

THE HIMALAYAS, the Andes, and the Alps are natural water reserves. They retain water from precipitation and ice in the wintertime, gradually releasing this water during the summertime. Global warming will cause the glaciers in these regions to melt too quickly and this will increase the water levels in rivers and lakes, causing floods. Even though natural floods have always occurred in nature and play a beneficial role, the floods that result from climate change have a negative impact on the wildlife population, on the environment, and on the lives of people, especially those who live in coastal areas.

AS CLIMATE change causes bodies of water like lakes, rivers, and oceans to become warmer, precipitation patterns begin to change. As a result, more frequent and more severe droughts occur. These affect crop production and access to water. A consequence of this is increased famine and the spread of disease.

POPULATIONS that inhabit the poorest areas in the world, like certain regions of Africa and Asia, will be more affected by higher temperatures.

RESPIRATORY problems will also affect people around the world, from Japan to Afghanistan and from China to Indonesia.

These problems are caused by pollutants from industries, thermoelectric power plants, and cars.

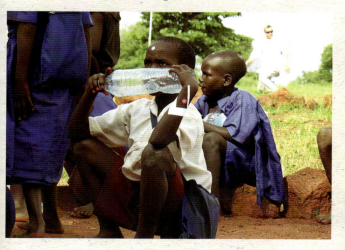

THE COMBINATION of floods in areas with poor drainage systems and heat waves will cause an increase in mosquito populations. This, of course, will cause diseases like dengue fever and malaria to spread in human populations.

Regardless of any technological progress we make now, we won't be able to escape the consequences of global warming.

Even if carbon dioxide emissions remained at the same levels they were in the year 2000, and even if no new industrial complexes were built nor another new cars were manufactured, Earth's average temperature would still rise about 0.1 °C per decade.

Is there anything we can do to change this?

What can we do to reduce GLOBAL

Humankind is indeed the main cause of global warming and the destruction of our natural habitat. What can we do to reduce the damage caused to nature and preserve the planet Earth for future generations?

THE DISCOVERY and widespread use of alternative energy sources are decisive in reducing or stopping one main global warming factor: CO_2 emissions.

Cars, buses, trucks, and airplanes are some of the main emitters of pollutants. Replacing gasoline with biofuels would help reduce greenhouse gas emissions.

Industries, households, and agriculture use large amounts of fossil fuels like petroleum and coal. Global warming could be diminished by using alternative energy sources such as:
- wind energy
- hydroelectric power plants
- solar energy
- geothermal energy
- wave and tidal energy

WARMING?

We live in an energy-rich world. Nature is constantly renewing this energy, but we need to learn to use it wisely.

Some countries such as Denmark, Germany, Spain, and the United States of America utilize financial support and other incentives to encourage companies and governments to invest in clean, renewable energy sources like wind, water, and the sun. These efforts have increased by 35% the use of wind and solar energy in some areas.

Besides searching for new sources of energy, we must rethink our habits, especially those related to energy and the ways we waste it.

WHERE WOULD THESE CHANGES HAPPEN?

In industries
- Producing more effective and long-lasting electrical equipment.
- Replacing conventional computer screens with LCD screens, which consume less energy, produce less heat and are made from recycled materials.

In agriculture and livestock
- Developing new technology to reduce CH_4 emissions from rice plantations and livestock.
- Constructing digesters that extract methane gas from livestock manure. These digesters produce biogas which could be used as fuel for vehicles, or as heat and electricity generators.
- Avoiding deforestation.

What else do we need to do?
- Use public transportation more often or ride a bike. We could also walk more.
- Reduce the use of private cars through tolled urban areas and greater taxation.
- Produce more environment-friendly vehicles.
- Use railroad transportation instead of cars and highways.

We can all help reduce global warming by changing some of our habits.

WE CAN START AT HOME:

1 Turn off the lights when you're not in a room.
2 Replace incandescent light bulbs with fluorescent ones.
3 Don't leave the tap running while brushing your teeth or shaving.
4 Avoid long showers.
5 Buy in-season organic food.
6 Cover the pan while cooking. You waste less energy and the cooking time is shorter.
7 Substitute your traditional electric oven for a microwave oven.
8 Turn off all electric equipment. Avoid leaving it on standby since you're using energy whenever the red or green light is on.
9 Install solar panels to heat water.
10 Don't press the button of two elevators simultaneously. And if you are going only one or two floors up or down, use the stairway.
11 When buying a car, consider flex-fuel models. Give your car regular checkups.
12 Check your car tires to make sure they are fully inflated.
13 Use public transportation. Walk or ride a bike. Try carpooling.
14 Plant trees and buy certified wood furniture only.
15 Adopt the 3Rs: Reduce, Reuse, and Recycle.
16 Don't burn trash and RECYCLE everything that can be recycled.

Para respostas e mais informações, acesse www.richmond.com.br.

PAGES 2 TO 7 QUESTIONS.

1. What is the natural phenomenon that maintains the Earth at an average temperature of 13 °C (55.4 °F)?
   a. greenhouse effect
   b. global warming
2. What is one of the main greenhouse gases?
   a. oxygen
   b. carbon dioxide
3. Which gas is given off during fossil fuel combustion?
   a. carbon dioxide
   b. oxygen
4. Which gas is naturally produced during the decomposition of organic matter?
   a. oxygen
   b. methane
5. Which of the following causes the depletion of the ozone layer?
   a. CO_2
   b. CFCs
6. What does the increase in the planet's average surface temperature cause?
   a. global warming
   b. greenhouse effect
7. Which gas is absorbed from the atmosphere during photosynthesis?
   a. carbon dioxide
   b. oxygen
8. What are some of the major pollutants?
   a. the combustion of fossil fuels and forest fires
   b. reforestation and photosynthesis
9. Which nation is the planet's major polluter?
   a. Russia
   b. Qatar
10. Which protocol tries to reduce the consumption and production of substances that deplete the ozone layer?
    a. Montreal Protocol
    b. Kyoto Protocol
11. Which protocol requires developed nations to reduce emissions of six greenhouse gases by 5.2% below the year 1990 levels?
    a. Montreal Protocol
    b. Kyoto Protocol
12. Which major polluter nation withdrew from the Kyoto Protocol in 2001?
    a. Russia
    b. the United States of America

PAGES 8 TO 13 QUESTIONS.

1. Which year was the warmest in the last 30 years?
   a. 2003
   b. 2004
   c. 2010
2. What short-term phenomenon does the melting of valley glaciers cause?
   a. hurricanes
   b. floods
   c. precipitation
3. A warmer global climate means more melting ice and an increase in...
   a. precipitation level
   b. river levels
   c. sea levels
4. What holds 9% of the planet's freshwater reserves?
   a. valley glaciers
   b. rivers
   c. lakes
5. Where is Larsen B platform located?
   a. the Himalayas
   b. the Antarctic Peninsula
   c. the Alps
6. How much of the Larsen B platform collapsed in 2002?
   a. less than 100 km^2
   b. between 500 km^2 and 1,000 km^2
   c. more than 2,000 km^2
7. What did this collapse cause?
   a. icebergs
   b. precipitation
   c. hurricanes
8. Which event may be linked to the rise in the average temperature of the sea over the last 30 years?
   a. droughts
   b. hurricanes
   c. floods
9. Which hurricane destroyed much of the American city of New Orleans?
   a. Katrina
   b. Rita
   c. Dennis

ASSIGNMENT

Research climate change and its impact on the region where you live. Pay attention to population growth, green area availability, rise in temperature, and increase in the number of vehicles and industries.

:: **PAGES 14 TO 17** CROSSWORD PUZZLE.

1 An island where we can find polar bears.
2 Polar bears are not only starving to death, they are also...
3 What colorful marine species may be one of the victims of global warming?
4 What do we call the phenomenon of corals expelling algae and looking like white skeletons?
5 Which greenhouse gas causes increased acidity in the ocean?
6 What is one forest that will be affected by the planet's temperature rise?
7 Which marine mammal feeds on krill, a type of small crustacean?
8 What do we call an area that is fish's natural nursery and guarantees its population replacement?

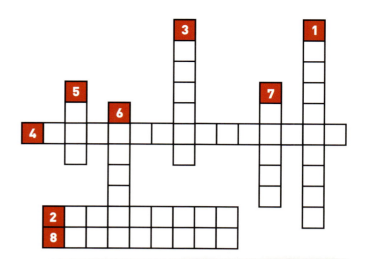

ASSIGNMENT
The Amazon Forest is an ecosystem with great biodiversity. Research two species of animals and two species of plants typically found in the Amazon.

:: **FIND NINE VOCABULARY TERMS RELATED TO GLOBAL WARMING IN THE BOX BELOW.**

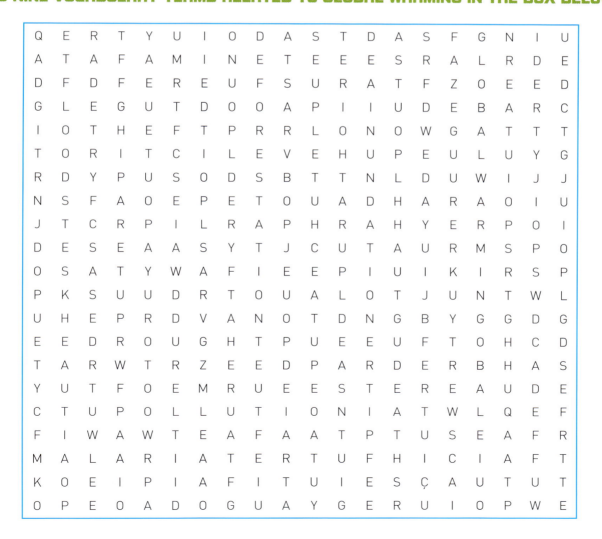

27

:: FIND OUT THE WORDS THAT ANSWER THE QUESTIONS BELOW.

1. What natural phenomenon provides the Earth with a warm temperature, which enables life to exist on land and in the oceans?

☐12 ☐14 ☐1 ☐1 ☐10 ☐15 ☐5 ☐7 ☐6 ☐1 ▨ ☐1 ☐2 ☐2 ☐1 ☐16 ☐4

2. Which greenhouse gas results from the decomposition of organic matter?

☐9 ☐1 ☐4 ☐15 ☐8 ☐10 ☐1

3. What activity leads to the destruction of forests due to tree cutting?

☐11 ☐1 ☐2 ☐5 ☐14 ☐1 ☐6 ☐4 ☐8 ☐4 ☐3 ☐5 ☐10

4. What event can cause floods?

☐9 ☐1 ☐13 ☐4 ☐3 ☐10 ☐12

5. What animals will have breathing difficulties due to increased water acidity?

☐2 ☐3 ☐6 ☐15

6. What living creature will undergo a bleaching process?

☐16 ☐5 ☐14 ☐8 ☐13

7. What must we preserve to ensure the survival of life on Earth?

☐10 ☐8 ☐4 ☐7 ☐14 ☐1

:: FIND THE HIDDEN MESSAGE BY FILLING OUT THE DIAGRAM WITH THE NUMBERED LETTERS FROM THE PREVIOUS ACTIVITY.

W																		
1	8	14	1		3	10	11	1	1	11		4	15	1		9	8	3	10

Row 2: 16 8 7 6 8 4 3 — 1 — V 8 12 1 10 4 6 — 5 2

Row 3: 12 13 5 — B 8 13 — W 8 14 9 3 10 12 .

Row 4: W 15 8 4 — 6 15 5 7 13 11 — W 1 — 11 5 — 4 5

Row 5: 14 1 11 7 16 1 — 4 15 1 — 11 8 9 8 12 1 — 4 5

Row 6: 10 8 4 7 14 1 — 8 10 11 — 15 1 13 — P P 14 1 6 1 14 — V 1

Row 7: 4 15 1 — P 13 8 10 1 4 — 2 5 14 — 2 7 4 7 14 1

Row 8: 12 1 10 1 14 8 4 3 5 10 6 ?

WRITE T (TRUE) OR F (FALSE).

1. (   ) Deforestation does not contribute to global warming.

2. (   ) We are accountable for the global warming issue and we need to find effective solutions to avoid a big environmental catastrophe.

3. (   ) Antarctica is the only place where we can see climate change already having an impact on the environment.

4. (   ) There is nothing we can do to prevent the average temperature of the planet from rising 0.1 °C per decade.

5. (   ) The populations of China and India are not subject to experience shortages of food because there is no effect of global warming on these regions.

:: YOU ARE A SCIENTIST... Carry out an experiment!

Materials

- TWO IDENTICAL GLASSES WITH THE SAME AMOUNT OF WATER IN THEM
- ALUMINUM FOIL
- A LARGE SHOEBOX
- A PAIR OF SCISSORS
- PVC FILM
- A THERMOMETER

What to do
1. Cover the inside of the shoebox with the aluminum foil and place one glass of water inside of it.
2. Cover the top of the box with the PVC film.
3. Place the box and the second glass of water in sunlight or under a lamp.
4. Wait 10 minutes. Measure the temperature of the water in both glasses.
5. Record the temperatures and compare your results.

Point to ponder
Which water sample is warmer? Formulate a hypothesis for this experiment.
Tip: Compare your results to the greenhouse effect.

:: YOU ARE A JOURNALIST...
Write a newspaper article!

FIND OUT THE LATEST NEWS ABOUT GLOBAL WARMING SO YOU CAN WRITE AN ARTICLE ABOUT IT. YOU CAN CHECK THE WEBSITES BELOW:

www.bbc.co.uk
www.topics.nytimes.com
www.nwf.org

:: YOU ARE AN ENVIRONMENTALIST...
Inform the population about global warming!

MAKE PAMPHLETS AND DISTRIBUTE THEM TO YOUR PEERS AT SCHOOL. PROVIDE TIPS ON WAYS TO GO GREEN AND MINIMIZE GLOBAL WARMING.

YOU CAN ALSO DESIGN AND WEAR A T-SHIRT TO BRING ATTENTION TO THE ISSUE.

:: YOU ARE A MUSICIAN...
Sing it all out!

YOU HAVE BEEN HIRED TO WRITE THE LYRICS TO A SONG ABOUT GLOBAL WARMING. THIS SONG WILL BE USED TO TELL THE WORLD ABOUT AN ENVIRONMENTAL NGO (NON-GOVERNMENTAL ORGANIZATION).

:: GLOSSARY

abatement = reduction
acidity = the state of being acid
amount = quantity
availability = the quality of being at hand when needed
average = the value obtained by dividing the sum of a set of quantities by the number of quantities in the set
below = underneath
bleaching = making white
cattle = a collective noun for cows and bulls
cement = a substance used in concrete
century = a period of 100 years
change = difference
cloud = condensed watery vapor in the sky
coal = a fossil fuel consisting of carbonized vegetable matter
coast = seashore, beach
collapsed = broke off, fell down
concern = worry
coral reef = a reef composed mainly of coral and other organic matter which have solidified into limestone
crop production = agricultural production of things growing from the ground
crustacean = arthropods such as lobsters, crabs, shrimps, and barnacles
danger = risk
deforestation = the removal of trees
degree = level
deplete = reduce
depletion = reduction
desertification = the process by which an area becomes a desert
developing = not yet highly industrialized
die out = disappear

disease-carrying = which carries sicknesses
doubt = question
drainage = the drying of land by removing the moisture
drop = fall
drought = dry weather
drown = die by submersion in water
due to = because of
Earth = the planet we live on
environmental = related to the natural environment, its protection and conservation
expel = kick out, get rid of
feed = give food or energy
flood = inundation
fossil fuel = a fuel formed from the remains of once-living organisms
given off = produced
global warming = increase in the average temperature of the Earth's surface
Great Barrier Reef = the largest coral reef in the world
greenhouse effect = the warming effect of the Earth's atmosphere
gross volume = total amount
growth = increase
heat = hot, a form of energy that is transferred by a difference in temperature
heat wave = a wave of unusually hot weather
hunting = the pursuit and killing of food
hurricane = a tropical cyclone or a violent storm
ice shelf = a thick mass of ice that is attached to land and floats over a large area of sea
increase = rise
infectious = transmissible from one being to another

issue = subject, problem
lake = a body of water surrounded by land
land = the solid part of the Earth's surface
landfill = a large outdoor area for waste disposal
landslide = the movement of earth down a steep slope
layer = a thickness of a material covering a surface or forming an overlying part or segment
lethal = deadly
main polluter = main contaminator
mangrove = a tropical or subtropical vegetation typical of tidal swamps
melting = a change of state from solid to liquid
mosquito-borne disease = a disease transmitted by mosquitoes
noticeable = detectable
nursery = an estuary where young fish grow up
organic matter = materials and debris that originated as living plants or animals
overall = total
ozone layer = a layer in Earth's atmosphere that absorbs considerable amounts of ultraviolet radiation and prevents heat loss from the planet
plain = a low flat area
plant matter = plants, vegetable material
polyp = an organism with a body shaped like a tube that has its mouth and tentacles on one end and is sealed on the other
pose = present

precipitation = rain
quarter = 1/4
random = accidental, aleatory
rate = speed
reasonable = logical
regardless = in spite of
release = free
reserve = a supply of something saved for future use
rise = increase
role = part
scarce = rarely encountered
sea = ocean
slowly = not quickly, without speed
spot = place
spread = propagation
status = situation
target = goal
threat = menace
treaty = a formal written agreement between countries or governments
trend = tendency
undergo = experience
unfairly = without justice
valley glacier = a large, long-lasting river of ice that is formed in valleys
vulnerable = less able to resist
warmer = hotter, more heated
weak = not strong
wetland = an area that is saturated by surface or ground water such as a swamp or bog
wildlife = wild animal population
withdrew = removed itself from
witness = see
wood = the solid material derived from woody plants, notably trees

Richmond

Richmond
First Floor
4 King Street Cloisters
Albion Place, London W6 0QT

Publisher: Paul Berry
Editorial Manager: Sandra Possas
Development Editor: Veronica Teodorov
Assistant Editor: Carolina Martins
Text: Lilia Regina Simões Menezes Bentiviegna
Translation: Leika Procopiak
Technical Adviser: Daniella A. Barroso
Proofreading: Katia Gouveia Vitale, Rafael Gustavo Spigel, Roberta Moratto Risther, Susan Banman Sileci
Design: Christiane Borin, Banana Biônica Design
Assistant Designer: Hulda Melo
Illustration: Estúdio Manga/Marco Aurélio, Daniel Brito
Picture Research: Rosana Carneiro
Cover: Banana Biônica Design/Marco Cançado

All rights reserved. No part of this book may be reproduced, stored in a retrieval system or transmitted in any form, electronic, mechanical, photocopying, or otherwise without the prior permission in writing of the publishers.

Dados Internacionais de Catalogação na Publicação (CIP)
(Câmara Brasileira do Livro, SP, Brasil)

Learn about global warming. — São Paulo : Moderna, 2007.

1. Aquecimento global – Estudo e ensino.

07-10300   CDD-551.525307

Índice para catálogo sistemático:

1. Aquecimento global : Estudo e ensino
551.525307

ISBN: 978-85-16-05761-9

© Editora Moderna, 2007

Richmond
Editora Moderna Ltda.
Rua Padre Adelino, 758 – Belenzinho
São Paulo – SP – Brasil – CEP 03303-904
Central de atendimento ao usuário:
0800 771 8181
www.richmond.com.br
2014
Impresso no Brasil

Photographs: Krill © Flip Nicklin/Minden Pictures/Latinstock; Satellite images of Larsen B platform desintegration, 2002 © NASA/Godard Space Flight Center Visualization Studio/ SPL/ Latinstock; Monte Everest © Brad Wrobleski/Masterfile/Other Images; People in flooded area, Rhine River, Kehl, Germany © Olivier Morin/AFP/Getty Images; Girl in hospital © Ian Boddy/SPL/Latinstock; Hurricane Rita in Havana, Cuba 09/2005 © Enrique de la Osa / epa / Corbis – Latinstock; PVC film © Paulo Manzi; Coral reef © Jupter Images; Golden frog © Michael Patricia Fogden / Minden Pictures – Latinstock; Great barrier reef in Australia © Ken Ross / Getty Images; all other images are royalty free.

Sources:

[1] Based on <www.profesorenlinea.cl/Ciencias/Efecto_invernadero.htm>. Accessed on January 21, 2014.

[2] <www.periodistadigital.com/ciencia/medioambiente/2013/09/27/onu-ipcc-temperatura-cambio-climatico-nivel-del-mar.shtml>. Accessed on January 23, 2014.

[3] <http://datos.bancomundial.org/indicador/EN.ATM.CO2E.PC>. Accessed on January 22, 2014.

[4] <http://unfccc.int/portal_espanol/informacion_basica/protocolo_de_kyoto/items/6215.php>. Accessed on January 23, 2014.

[5] Adapted from <www.bbc.co.uk/news/science-environment-20653018l>. Accessed on January 23, 2014.

[6] <http://ummundoglobal.blogspot.com.br/2011/01/2010-confirmado-no-topo-dos-anos-mais.html#!/2011/01/2010-confirmado-no-topo-dos-anos-mais.html>. Accessed on January 22, 2014.

[7] Based on <www.esa.int/por/ESA_in_your_country/Portugal/Satelite_capta_desintegracao_de_gelo_na_Antartida>. Accessed on January 22, 2014.

[8] <www.skepticalscience.com/sea-level-rise-predictions.htm>. Accessed onJanuary 22, 2014.

[9] <http://eradicatehunger.org/pdf/Anti_Hunger_ES.pdf>. Accessed on January 23, 2014.

[10] <http://cienciasycosas.wordpress.com/2011/03/26/huracanes-terremotos-y-cambio-climatico/>; <www.monografias.com/trabajos52/cambio-climatico/cambio-climatico2.shtml>. Accessed on January 23, 2014.

[11] <http://waste.ideal.es/cambioclimatico11.htm>. Accessed on January 23, 2014.

[12] <www.bbc.co.uk/mundo/noticias/2012/10/121002_arrecife_gran_barrera_perdida_am.shtml>. Accessed on January 23, 2014.